Daddy is Cool
Like That

By Mary Anne McMahon and Jennifer Bucciero Boyles

Illustrated by Ros Webb

Illustrations by Ros Webb

ISBN

Dedicated to Michael George Bucciero

1944 - 2021

A person can have more degrees than a thermometer, but one lesson in the school of hard knocks tops them all.

Michael George Bucciero

John Paul,
Stay Cool Like That,

Prologue

This book is a love letter to my dad, Michael George Bucciero, who passed away on June 18, 2021. Enduring multiple sclerosis for many years was not an easy task, but my dad found enjoyment in life and was a good role model for my sister and me. Discovering that my father had MS as a young child was incredibly devastating. I just wanted him to be normal like other dads. I went through a range of emotions as described in this book—sad, scared, embarrassed, angry—until I finally reached acceptance. I equate it to the stages of grief. I had to mourn the loss of the father he could have been and accept the one right in front of me.

I grew up admiring his laid-back disposition and how he kept a positive attitude through many challenges. I am grateful for the years I shared with him. While I watched friends lose healthy fathers, my dad forged ahead. I wish that he never had to suffer from such a debilitating disease, but his struggle taught me many things. His best lesson was to keep going no matter what. My dad had fun, told jokes, lived large, and always had a big smile on his face.

My Daddy was cool like that.

Though this book is not exactly my story, it is based on some of my personal experiences and my own childhood emotions of having a disabled parent. I hope this story can help other children deal with the emotional trauma of having a disabled parent and can inspire them to appreciate life no matter what comes their way. I believe that my dad will always be remembered by his friends and family for his wit, his incessant reading, his love of music, and, later, for his alternative ways to continue a joyful life. He was valued and will be missed by everyone who knew him.

Jennifer Bucciero Boyles

After finishing her homework, Rachael kept peeking out the kitchen window so she would know the minute when Daddy got home from work. They played tag in the backyard every Tuesday. Then they ate dinner and afterward Daddy would always take Rachael and her little sister, Laura, to the ice cream shop.

"Get whatever you want!" he'd say.

Rachael and Laura would always choose a big banana split with three scoops of ice cream, hot fudge, sprinkles, and a cherry on top.

Daddy is cool like that.

Finally, Rachael saw her mom hurrying outside to help Daddy out of his white convertible sports car.

"Are you okay, Daddy?" Rachael asked when he entered the house.

"I feel a little tired today, Rachael. I can't play tag."

Rachael was sad, but she wanted Daddy to take care of himself and get better. So, she gave him a big hug. She knew there wasn't going to be any tag or ice cream tonight, but that was all right.

On Saturday, Rachael cleaned her room so she and Daddy could play on the slide at the neighborhood park like they always did on Saturday.

When she went into the kitchen for breakfast her mom said that she was taking Daddy to the doctor on Monday. Rachael then realized that Daddy was still too sick to play with her. He needed to rest some more.

Sometimes she and Daddy went to the movies on Saturday afternoon. Afterward he would order two pizzas. One pizza had pineapple on it! Daddy always said that the great thing about pizza is that it could be eaten for breakfast, lunch, or dinner. On Sunday they ate cold pizza for breakfast and warm pizza for lunch and dinner. Rachael wondered if she and Daddy would ever have fun like that again.

When Rachael got off the school bus on Monday, Daddy was standing with crutches under his arms.

Daddy asked everyone to come inside the house. He sounded so serious. When they were all sitting around the kitchen table, he said that he had multiple sclerosis. He said that MS, as some people call it, can keep people from walking.

"How does multiple sclerosis do that?" Rachael asked.

Daddy told her that multiple sclerosis attacks the nerves in a person's body. When a person's nerves don't work correctly, the legs become too weak to walk on.

Rachael knew that if her dad could not walk or stand, he could not play tag or play on the slide ever again. She burst into tears.

"Don't cry, Rachael," Laura said. "Daddy can still crawl with us."

Rachael clenched her hands into tight balls.

"You don't understand anything!" she yelled and then ran to her bedroom.

A few minutes later her mom knocked on her
bedroom door and came in.

"Mommy, I'm scared!" Rachael shouted.

"I know, honey. Daddy's MS is scary, but we
will get through this together."

Rachael wondered what her friends would say
when they saw her dad on crutches. Would
they make fun of him? She didn't want Daddy
to be different from other dads. Rachel's
stomach started to hurt and tears streamed
down her cheeks.

On Tuesday Dad went to have some tests done at the hospital. When Rachael got home from school Laura and Grandmother Grace were sitting on the front porch. She sat down beside them.

Grandmother Grace gave her a big hug. "I love both of you girls very much. I will be here with you anytime Mommy has to take Daddy to doctor appointments."

A few minutes later Rachael's mom drove into the driveway in her blue SUV. She quickly got out of the SUV and pulled out a wheelchair from the back of her SUV. Grandmother Grace jumped up and helped Daddy out of the vehicle and over to the wheelchair. Her Mom and Grandmother then slowly placed Daddy into the wheelchair.

Rachael could not believe her eyes. Only a week ago her dad had started having trouble walking, and now he was in a wheelchair. Her stomach began to hurt again, but she tried hard not to cry in front of her dad.

That night Rachael cried herself to sleep, but in the morning, she put on a smile when she saw Daddy. Laura was giggling and sitting on his lap. Laura was only four and didn't understand that MS is a serious condition. But Rachael was eight, and she knew better.

During breakfast Daddy told them that he was going to the hospital for therapy so that he could get stronger. The people there would teach him to operate his wheelchair and do tasks while he was sitting in it. Rachael wondered if Daddy has to be in a wheelchair will he ever be the same again.

The next day Mom called Laura and Rachael into the kitchen and told them that they would all be getting some therapy.

"Why?" Rachael asked. "We can walk okay."

"Will we learn how to push Daddy in his wheelchair?" Laura asked.

Mom explained to Rachael and Laura that they would be getting a different kind of therapy. They would talk to someone about Daddy's MS.

"We will learn how to deal with our sadness over Daddy's disability," Mom said. "We will talk about how we feel and will learn not to be afraid of Daddy's differences. The therapist will help us remember that Daddy can still be fun and show us ways to have a good time with him in a wheelchair."

"That will never happen!" Rachael shouted.

"Rachael, we'll still like playing with him," Laura said.

"You might like playing with him. I won't!" Rachael felt like she was going to cry again. She ran to her bedroom and hugged her doll, Patty. Patty always made her feel better when she was upset.

Both Patty and Daddy are cool like that.

Later, Rachael learned that her mother was right. The therapist did help her feel better about Daddy's MS. Rachael noticed that she didn't have stomachaches anymore, and she didn't cry as much.

After several weeks of therapy Daddy came home. "I'm as strong as a bull now," he said with a big smile.

He explained that his therapist helped him gain arm muscle. Now he could lift himself from his wheelchair onto the couch, into his bed, and into his new mobility scooter. Daddy's new scooter had a button that could make it go slow or fast. Daddy rode the scooter as fast as a bicycle. Soon Laura and Rachael were having fun riding the scooter, too. Daddy even let the neighborhood kids ride the scooter.

Daddy got a handicap license plate and added some handicap features to his white convertible, but then later decided that he needed a more handicap friendly vehicle. He traded in his convertible for a cool new red SUV with fancy seats, a wheelchair lift, and a TV. When Daddy pushed on a handlebar the SUV drove just like if he was stepping on a gas pedal. When he pushed the other bar, the brakes stopped the SUV.

The driver's seat could turn all the way around to let Daddy lift himself out of his wheelchair and into the driver's seat. Sometimes Laura and Rachael twirled around in the driver's seat, too. After everyone buckled their seatbelts, Daddy would take them for a ride. They liked sitting up high in the new van. Sometimes Daddy even let Rachael and Laura ride up and down on his van's lift.

Daddy played music while he drove and he always asked, "Hey girls, what's on TV?" Then Rachael and Laura would find a fun movie. Daddy liked listening to music and movies at the same time!

Loving loud music is one thing that MS did not change about Daddy. At home he still played his favorite songs for many hours while Rachael and Laura danced to the music. Daddy always hated dancing. He just loved sitting and listening to the songs.

Daddy is cool like that.

Slide Saturday turned into Splash Saturday when Daddy started taking the girls to the neighborhood pool. Daddy's arms were so strong from therapy that he could swim in the pool just using his arms. Daddy swam next to the girls and taught them how to do the crawl stroke. He showed them how to move their arms and lift their face out of the water at the right time to breathe.

Rachael and Laura often went to the grocery store with Daddy. Rachael sometimes felt embarrassed because they were the only kids in the store with a wheelchair dad, but then Daddy would start telling funny jokes. Everyone in the store would laugh and then Rachael wouldn't feel embarrassed anymore. Soon Rachael realized that Daddy was still fun. She and Laura had to do grown-up jobs like reach for items on shelves and put bags full of groceries into the van, but they liked helping Daddy.

When they finished buying healthy food Daddy always said, "It's junk food time. Pick out some treats."

Rachael often chose Daddy's favorite chocolate cake mix. When she got home, she made the cake for him. She wanted to make Daddy happy.

"Get some big yellows and put them in the cake," he would say. That meant he wanted lots of bananas between the layers of cake.

After Rachael covered the cake with chocolate frosting Daddy always said, "Can you give me the biggest slice, please?"

When he finished eating, he would shout, "This cake is **DELICIOUS**!!"

Daddy is cool like that.

Grandmother Grace suggested that they get Daddy a service dog to help him with tasks and keep him company. So, one Sunday afternoon the whole family went to look at service dogs.

When they arrived at the Super Service Dog Kennel Laura ran right to a Golden Labrador Retriever.

"Daddy, we need to get this dog!" she shouted.

The woman helping them smiled. "This little girl knows how to pick out a dog. Tammy is our best dog. She is smart, kind, and helpful."

When Tammy was introduced to Daddy, she jumped onto his lap. Daddy took her for a wheelchair ride. Tammy licked Daddy's face and wagged her tail. Rachael and Laura just laughed and laughed! Tammy and Daddy were a match.

"This dog is **MAGNIFICENT**!" Daddy shouted.

Tammy is cool like Daddy.

The next Sunday a dog trainer came to their house and taught Tammy how to help their dad with tasks around the house. The trainer told everyone that Tammy was a fast learner and would be a loyal pet. He was correct.

Sometimes Daddy threw balls to Tammy in the backyard. She almost always caught them. Then Rachael and Laura began tossing balls to Tammy with their dad. Tag Tuesday was now called Toss Tuesday. Like Tammy, Rachel and Laura began to enjoy playing with Daddy in his wheelchair.

Sometimes getting the morning newspaper was challenging for Daddy. So, Tammy started running out every morning to grab the paper in her mouth. Then she brought it to Daddy. Tammy followed Daddy around everywhere, and if he dropped something, she picked it up. Tammy got excited when Daddy did a new task by himself. She would wag her tail and bark! Tammy taught Rachael and Laura how important it was to help their dad and cheer him on when he did a good job in his wheelchair.

Rachael and Laura wanted Tammy to join them at the pool. Their mother talked to the lifeguard, and he agreed to allow Tammy to come to the pool early in the morning before it was open to everyone else. So, on the next Splash Saturday, Tammy came with them to the pool! Once at the pool Tammy just stood next to it. She was scared to go into the water. Their dad gently patted Tammy on her head. Tammy jumped in and swam across the pool and back. Daddy then barked three times. Tammy knew that barks meant success because that was what she was trained to do when Daddy did a task correctly. Rachael and Laura could not believe their eyes! Now Daddy was helping Tammy.

"Tammy is **AMAZING**!" Daddy shouted.

That Saturday Tammy stayed in the pool and swam with Daddy until it was time to go home.

Daddy and Tammy are cool like that.

At the end of the summer the whole family and Grandmother Grace went to the girls' favorite amusement park. Laura and Rachael learned that having a dad in a wheelchair could be a big advantage. Because of their dad's disability, they were allowed to go to the front of the line and be the first to get on each ride.

One little boy even told Rachael and Laura, "Your dad is so cool. You are lucky. Everyone at the park treats you special."

The boy was right. The amusement park was much more fun when you weren't waiting in line, and besides Daddy was the most fun dad in the whole park.

While at the park Daddy kept saying, "Let's boogie!" That meant "Let's go on some more rides!"

Daddy is cool like that.

Rachael and Laura now understood many things. If Daddy hadn't gotten into a wheelchair, Tammy would never have come to live with them. They liked living with her. They all had so much fun together throwing balls in the backyard and swimming at the pool. Rachael and Laura were treated like princesses at the amusement park. They got to ride up high in a really cool van and ride fast on Daddy's mobility scooter. All because Daddy had a disability.

The two girls learned that some earlier activities didn't have to end because Daddy had MS. Daddy still played loud music and told silly jokes, and now Rachael and Laura got the biggest ice cream sundaes at the ice cream shop. He still bought them hot pizzas on Saturday, and the whole family ate cold pizza with pineapple for breakfast and warm pizza for lunch and dinner on Sunday.

Daddy is still so cool.

Thank-you Daddy for always smiling and uplifting our spirits.

Made in the USA
Middletown, DE
19 April 2022

64424970R00020